the
joy
leaving

sh*t
of

all

your
the

place

over

the jo

the

leavin

sh*t al

The Countryman Press
A division of W. W. Norton & Company
Independent Publishers Since 1923

the pl

jennifer mccartney

For information about permission to reproduce
selections from this book, write to Permissions,
The Countryman Press, 500 Fifth Avenue,
New York, NY 10110

For information about special discounts for bulk
purchases, please contact W. W. Norton
Special Sales at specialsales@wwnorton.com
or 800-233-4830

The Countryman Press
www.countrymanpress.com

A division of W. W. Norton & Company, Inc.
500 Fifth Avenue, New York, NY 10110
www.wwnorton.com

978-1-58157-387-9

10 9 8 7 6 5 4 3 2 1

author's note

This is not a book about tidying. It's not about
how to organize your life. Or about how to
become joyful. It's not a self-help book, either. It
can't help you determine the color of your parachute or find the power of now. It's a parody.
That's why you found it in the humor section.
Or the humour section, if you're in Canada.

contents

how do you
even draw a
typewriter?

Introduction

"Whenever you find yourself on the side of the majority, it is time to pause and reflect."
—MARK TWAIN

Tidy is in. Messy is out. Thanks, minimalism. Thanks, unprecedented household debt. Thanks, KonMari Method.[1]

My friends and family fell enthusiastically under the influence of the twelve billion-copy bestseller, *The Life-Changing Magic of Tidying Up,* and they all failed, time and again. It's an ugly thing to witness. Oh, you wish you hadn't thrown out your grandmother's crocheted bikini or your son's ashtray he made in the shape of a leg of lamb? Too fucking bad. They're gone, thanks to your weird ideas about tidying.

Break free from the bonds of tidiness and triumph over the boring forces of uniformity and predictability. Every tidy home looks the same—particularly when there's nothing left in it—but a messy home, now that's a better way

....

1. It's okay I guess if you don't know about this (of course it's sort of weird if you don't), but in short, it's about talking to your socks.

to live. Better, more honorable, and truer to the American Dream in so many ways.

America is the land of opportunity, and the land of acquisition. Canada even more so because of all the snow-related accessories. "Get rid of your stuff" is a ridiculous suggestion. It's cowardly, too. Sure, it's easier to go through your drawers and randomly throw away all your shit—sorry, *selectively keep the shit you feel joyful about*—than it is to deal with whatever bullshit week you're having. But isn't it better to deal with your problems and not blame shit, as if the reason you're not getting more oral sex has to do with your husband's massive tie collection? Cleaning is the easy way out. Do not be seduced by that. (But before you deal with your problems, let's try solving them quickly by firing up your laptop and buying three or more things to make yourself feel better.)

Everyone likes to buy things and inherit things and collect things, and have said things around. Science has even proven that having a lot of stuff makes you more open to new ideas, more creative, and (obviously) smarter. A study published in *Psychological Science* "discovered" that "disorderly environments encourage breaking with tradition and convention"—the people in the messy rooms came up with almost five times the number of highly creative responses as did their tidy-room counterparts and were also more likely to choose smoothie flavors that were labeled as "new" as opposed to "classic."[2] This is true. Do not be hung up on being tidy. Think about all the fruits you could be tasting if you were just a little bit messier. Or think about the limited time you have on this planet before you

smoothie

2. Vohs, Kathleen D., Joseph P. Redden, and Ryan Rahinel. "Physical Order Produces Healthy Choices, Generosity, and Conventionality, Whereas Disorder Produces Creativity," Psychological Science 24, no. 9 (2013).

die of Zika virus or from unwashed spinach or, let's face it, probably heart disease.

Just how fucking dedicated must you be to a tidy abode? Have you been brainwashed into believing that wanting to have shit, and not worrying where it goes, means there's something wrong with you? That you ought to be devastated if you and your place will never be featured on *Goop* or *Martha Stewart Living* or *Apartment Therapy*? Reject the KonMari mindset; it will only bring shame and guilt upon your household when you ultimately fail.

And here's the biggest load of crap: that being tidy will actually improve your emotional life. Anger issues? Too much stuff. Unhappy marriage? Too much stuff. Can't sleep? Stuff! Problems with your digestion? It's not gluten— it's all your fucking stuff. Look, you know who was very tidy? Patrick Bateman, the serial murderer, from *American Psycho*. Also, Mussolini was a very tidy man. He *loved* filing papers. Ted

Bundy? Neat as fuck. Now ask yourself, what kind of company do you want to keep?

In this book, I'm going to provide you with my own system for living a full life, called the FREE Method. It stands for nothing. Frozen Rogaine Eggs Eggs? Fancy Riding Eve Ensler? Sure. But freedom is amazing and we should all strive for it; otherwise we'll end up fapping our lives away like the FAPpers (Fatally Addicted to Purging [your belongings, not your lunch]). In this book, I will help you transform your life so that you'll never struggle with cleanliness again. I will break you of the urge to tidy as hard as Tonya Harding's goons whacked Nancy Kerrigan's kneecap. Throwback reference.

It's time for FAP deprogramming. Some of the KonMari guidelines should make you shudder (if you're a person who is alive and not susceptible to cults, anyway). With this handy chart, I'll compare and contrast the beliefs of the FAPs and the FREE.

	FAP	FREE
Books that you love to read	Books are clutter. Tear out only the pages you like and keep them in a file. Recycle the rest.	Don't be a fucking idiot.
Old baking dish that reminds you of your mother and childhood tuna casseroles	Ditch it. Who needs Mom? Your mother isn't actually a casserole dish. Get it?	Are you still making tuna casseroles? You'll need a dish for that, lovely Midwestern housewife from 1970.
All of your socks	You only need a few pairs of socks, and you should roll them carefully into little swirls. If you fold them any other way you're kind of an idiot and your socks will be sad.	Socks don't have feelings.

Not only do FAPpers require their followers to toss out most of their worldly possessions, keeping only possessions that arouse them—I mean, *spark pleasure*—followers are also encouraged to talk to those items. Do you have time to empty your purse every day, fold it, place it on a shelf, and thank it for its service?

Let's all chill the fuck out.

DISCLAIMER:
SELF-HELP BOOKS ARE BULLSHIT.

....

Books don't solve problems. Alcohol can help and drugs are certainly a good solution, but *what color is your parachute?* Really? Can you learn to think like a man? Win friends and influence people? Harness the power of now? Fuck off. Even established self-help books like the Bible, the Quran, and the Book of Mormon (based on the popular Broadway play) are still limited in their ability to solve all your problems because they are fucking books. **Books don't fix you. I am not promising to fix you. Indeed, my goal is to destroy any desire you have to help yourself or anyone you know, especially when that desire comes in the form of being neat and tidy, which, let's face it, is a passing desire most of the time anyway.**

I know you're always looking for the easy fix, the magic bullet. So am I. But I know from experience that cults are not the answer. Sex parties are not the answer. Nor are any of the pre-organized-religion-yet-still-kind-of-religious concepts that are making a comeback. Astrology. Crystals. Tarot Cards. Wicca. Magic 8-Balls. Yoga. The Container Store. It's okay to want someone else to steer the ship a bit. It's normal to want answers to shit like, "Why does his dick look weird—is it an STD?" or "How many personal essays about my bulimia do I have to publish on *Huffington Post* before I get a book deal?" or "Why did I get married?"[3] I get why self-help books are popular and why you pray to L. Ron Hubbard and why cooking contests and real estate shows are broadcast 36 times a day. It's weirdly satisfying to see people

....

3. This was legitimately the fifth Google Autocomplete result when I typed "why," which is super depressing.

on television fuck up but then also get all their shit together. Same thing with seeing someone make an amazing rose petal cake out of meringue and baby panda's breath. There's nothing wrong with wanting to improve your station in life or making changes to things you're unhappy with, I guess. But be wary of neat slogans and books that promise life-changing magic. The only real magic in the world is from unicorns and the high you get from poppers.

I'm kind of a big deal

Messiness is easy. It comes naturally to everyone. You're born fucking messy and you die messy but someplace in between you get brainwashed into thinking that you should be tidy. No one likes tidy people. They are boring. Basically even writing a book about being messy is pointless because it's so fucking easy. But here we are.

I will show you how to renounce the cult-like devotion to tidiness and I will change your life. **When you are messy, everything else in your life will fall into place.** Your study will be accepted into *Scientific American*. Your plants will stop dying. Your whisky bottle will never run dry. Your Duane Reade and Shoppers Drug Mart points will finally add up to a free jar of salsa and some nice shampoo. Your Facebook post about motherhood will go viral.

How can I promise you this? I've spent the last [redacted] years of my life being messy. Ask my mother. Or my university housemates that kept passive-aggressively highlighting my name on the chores sheet and leaving me notes under my door like *DISHES!* and then doing my dishes anyway 40 seconds later because they were pretty uptight. I spend a lot of time traveling to my friends' houses and leaving my sweaty Coronas on their wooden coffee tables. I've spilled nail polish upon multiple surfaces across many states. I display collections of beach rocks and piggy banks and political bobbleheads and men in an apartment that doesn't even fit a full-size fridge. I have Archie Comics and My Little Ponies in a box under the bed. Two hundred and fifty My Little Ponies.[4] Despite society's best efforts to make me feel guilty about all of this, I don't. I am a messy person. I'm very good at it. And so are you—but you already know this. In this book, I will liberate you from the daily bull-

....

4. I was an only child so I was spoiled but also so lonely I played with plastic horses.

shit of FAPing so that you, too, can live a life of mess and glamour.

But don't just listen to me.

Here are some testimonials from happy clients who email me constantly to say things like:

- I finally succeeded in finishing *Infinite Jest*.

- Kale tastes less bitter now that I've read your book.

- Thanks so much for teaching me how to not give a shit.

- Just spent 200 dollars at Sephora.

- My video installation won the Turner Prize.

- I can't find my shoes.

- My teeth are much whiter since I started your program.

- My husband is sleeping with the nanny.

And the list goes on.

My clients are so happy! Now it's time for the first step on the road to clutter. **Promise yourself to fucking cool it with the tidying.** Without this step, you cannot go any further. Probably. It's not an exact science.

1.

Reset your life by vowing never to tidy

"If a cluttered desk is a sign of a cluttered mind, of what, then, is an empty desk a sign?"

—ALBERT EINSTEIN

Being tidy is a tedious way to live, and no one wants to do it. That's why there are a hundred books about how to do it properly. You buy those books to feel good, but then you don't feel anything. There are no books about how to be messy because, guess what? It takes literally no effort and we're all really fucking good at it. I say, stick with what you're good at. But it's hard, in this culture of neatness and minimalism and tidiness. Instead of living your life, you're stressing about keeping your shit together.

You're not able to bake a decent-looking apple pie without Photoshopping it before posting on social media. Your manicure is chipped. You're just kind of generally muddling through. In order to get the kids to school on time, you skip blow-drying your hair. In order to pick up the dry cleaning, you skip your coffee before heading to your doctor's appointment. At your doctor's appointment you re-up your prescription for a bunch of anti-anxiety meds to help keep your anxiety in check. And the cycle continues.

This isn't about diagnosing or treating actual medical problems, obviously. This is a book, not WebMD. If you need meds, take them, obviously. Or take wine. But the point is that this low-level anxiety and guilt is a really boring way to expend your mental energy. You can get rid of it. And I can show you how.

All you need is a bottle of booze. Open, pour, drink. And do the following exercise:

Take a good look at your living room. Run through the mental checklist you've built up over the years relating to that space. Think about all the shit you've been meaning to do in this room. Does it need painting? Does it have enough midcentury furniture? Did your kid do a poo in the corner? Is there a canvas with a motivational saying that you've been meaning to hang up leaning against the wall, but you can't find a hammer, or the soles of your shoes aren't hard enough to serve as a hammer? Are there a bunch of terrible polemics your adjunct professor friends wrote on the coffee table that you've been meaning to read so you can face them at their next dinner party and be like, "What a meaningful exploration of femininity as it relates to the Samoan woodlouse"? Is the lamp shade dusty?

Now imagine not giving a fuck about any of it. I mean, *do* you actually give a fuck? If you were hooked up to a polygraph machine or super high, and someone asked you if you cared, what would you say? I'm guessing you don't actually care but you think you should care. Or you care what someone else would think if they saw the mess. If you want to do this new-age style, pretend this is some kind of mystic journey, courtesy of some ayahuasca and weed. Ready?

Grandma's crosstitch

HOME

BE FREE

....

Imagine this room as a beautiful landscape.
See the pile of unread magazines as a hill, see
the boots you keep meaning to sell on eBay but
can't seem to photograph without weird spots
showing up that aren't actually there as maybe
a couple of trees, see the couch with its blanket
and throw pillows and half-eaten bag of chips as
the sand and towels on a beach. Let go of caring,
let go of guilt and feelings of failure. Breathe
in good messy, breathe out boring tidy. Let it
slowly flow out of your body in one continu-
ous breath, or probably a few breaths, until you
no longer give any fucks. Imagine accepting this
room as it is. Imagine relinquishing your responsibility for this.

Maybe four months ago you sorted this entire room and were certain that every single item left in it brought you joy. Maybe four months ago you felt like life had changed for the better because you took a few bags of stuff to the charity shop. Perhaps you felt like you were turning over a new leaf. Guess what. **Your living room probably looks exactly the fucking same as it did before that deep clean, am I right? So fucking embrace it.** This is your natural state, sweetheart. You were born messy.

The more you buy, the messier you can be

This may seem counterintuitive. *Oh, I bought another cat so I should make more of an effort to be tidy with the ones I already have.* Nope. The more stuff you have, the more you've been liberated from any obligations to society (see the chapter on hoarding for proof of this). The more you've won the race to consume as much and as many resources as possible. The planet thanks you.

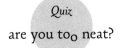

1. When you get home after a long trip the first thing you do is:

   A. unpack, transferring your neatly rolled clothing tubes from your suitcase into your closet, wash your hands eleven times, and put on some soothing jazz music while preparing yourself some fragrant green tea.

   B. put on your jogging pants and order pizza and watch 40 hours of Netflix until 6 a.m. Eat the pizza on paper plates. Being an adult is amazing.

   C. feed your cat.

2. In the bathroom, your soap and shampoo:

   A. are wiped dry after every use, and placed out of sight in the cupboard.

   B. sit on the side of the tub, open, mildewed, and ready for action.

C. don't exist. You don't use soap and shampoo because you're really into the no-poo method where everything is natural and chemical-free and can't harm your cats.

3. When you open your closet, you see:

A. your clothes, blessed with holy water and organized by category, with darker, cool-weather clothes on the left and light, warm-weather clothes on the right. God, what great friends you have in your clothes!

B. clean clothes hung on hangers, and dirty clothes on the ground. Shoes are usually under the dirty clothes.

C. your cats.

Answer Key:

Mostly As: **You have some issues. Read more of this book to learn how to chill out.**

Mostly Bs: **Congrats on being cool. On your death bed you'll be like, "It was worth it."**

Mostly Cs: **You probably like animals. Specifically, cats.**

Here are the last five things I bought:

1. Jane Kramer's *Lone Patriot*, a book about some militiamen who thought the New World Order was threatening their way of life and who decided to overthrow the US government. Spoiler: They were not successful.

2. A reading light, because my husband won't let me have the overhead light on until 4 a.m. while I finish my book about militiamen.

3. An air purifier, because New York is generally full of urine molecules and hipster effluent that must be filtered.

4. A new laptop case. It's gray and orange!

5. A fucking diptyque candle. I'm a grown-up and if I want a 60 dollar candle from France, what's it to you? They smell good and look pretty. Not that I can ever burn it. That'll cost me 10 bucks an hour and

then what am I left with? A headache from some overly perfumed wax and an empty glass jar to put makeup brushes or wooden matchsticks in.

And the best part is, I have no proper place to put any of it! Inspired? I thought so. Now it's your turn. Check out the resources section of this book, where I list a few excellent places to begin acquiring more things you don't have room for that will help you make a better mess.

Never discard anything

Here's a detailed breakdown of clutter strategies to employ. When I do content marketing or white papers for PR firms, I'll write stuff like, "By leveraging these strategies across all channels, the opportunity for growth is exponential." Here, I'll just say strategies like "always have booze in the house" and "don't talk to your clothing" will be helpful to learn if you want to be a normal person. The key is keeping every-thing in order to ward off regret later. My friend donated a bunch of her mom's clothing after she died, and 20 years later is kicking herself. Who wouldn't love a green pantsuit right now? And that's all stuff you can pass down to your own kids so they can wear it for Halloween and make fun of how fashion sucked back then and kind of shit all over your cherished memories of your mother because kids are assholes.

In doubt? Keep it. It doesn't bring you joy? Too bad. Probably because it's a fucking sweater and not a winning Powerball ticket. Make sense? Read on.

Save all booze. It never goes bad.

Having a well-stocked booze cabinet is handy for a number of reasons:

1. If you ever get the urge to tidy you can do a shot of vodka or drink a bottle of Tempra-nillo and remember/forget your priorities.

2. When your friend's pretentious boyfriend who got a book about whiskey for Christmas asks if you have any Japanese whisky, you can ask *from which prefecture* he'd prefer.

3. It's expected of normal adults.

Unless you're a recovering alcoholic or Mormon or have liver problems, you should always have booze in the house. We were once invited to an acquaintance's place for brunch and they offered us green tea and salad and it was a fucking nightmare. Obviously salad isn't a brunch food but whatever. Not having coffee is a pretty dick move—strike two. But, if you invite someone over, you better at least have a bottle of vodka in the freezer or some weird dark ale leftover from your last dinner party to offer your guests, or they will hate you. If you're still in college or whatever, just having a massive case of beer handy is acceptable. Preferably somewhere people will trip over it.

Keep lots of empty bags in your house

Plastic bags are great for storing stuff, so you should always have a lot of those on hand—empty or otherwise. Tote bags are also great. You can literally own 40 tote bags and it's never enough. I have tote bags from the Hoover Dam, a Turkish literary agency, and Niagara Falls. I also have totes with things like watermelons and geese on them. If you ever go to any event ever, for any reason, they will give you a tote bag. Medical conference? Tote bag. Wedding? Tote bag. Syrian refugee arriving in Canada? Maple leaf tote bag. My orthodontist gave me a tote bag. And a t-shirt. Which I put in the tote bag. And laundry bags and baskets should obviously always be full.

Keep paper relics for all time

I had a boss once who would open her mail and then rip it all into tiny pieces and recycle it like a maniac. It didn't matter what it was. Bills. Sentimental letters. Jury summons. She figured if

this is a love letter

it was really important the sender would call or email or send another letter. This strategy makes sense on the one hand, but on the other, this is a fucking terrifying way to live. Paper is meant to be collected and kept for all time. This is why I still have all the dragons my high school boy-friend drew me. And the mini golf score sheet from St. Ignace where I went with my Michi-gan boyfriend on our day off from work. More broadly, this includes old photographs, like the photobooth strips from your trips to the mall; every business card handed to you at awkward networking luncheons; your energy bills going back 10 years; engagement cards; sympathy cards; emails you printed back when you weren't sure how long the Internet was going to last; etc. When my parents moved from a house to a condo in 2012, we discovered every phone book

PILE THINGS TO MAKE
MORE ROOM FOR MORE STUFF

....

In their book, *A Perfect Mess*, Eric Abrahamson and David H. Freedman explain that "piles have a chronological meaning to them . . . people know how many inches they have to go down on a pile to get so many weeks or months back in time, and that makes it very easy to find things."

I don't need a book to tell me that. Mess piles are just good science. Every time you want to wear your favorite sweater, it's like going on an archeological dig. Remember when you wanted to be an archeologist? We all did. Because of dinosaurs. So, basically, by piling stuff in heaps, we're fulfilling a childhood dream.

going back to 1995 in my dad's office. This is how you do it. Keep it all and let your kids deal with it when you go. Hopefully not in a fiery inferno fueled by all your paper relics.

Don't overthink it. Your stuff doesn't have feelings.

a shirt with
feelings?
No

Your socks are not sad that they are balled up in your drawer. Your sweater is not sad that it's on the floor. Your bag is not sad that you didn't thank it for its service today. If these things were true, your shoes would be sad that you're walking on them all the time and your jeans would be like, please don't keep sitting on me or at least wash me once in a while, for fuck's sake. Normal people have enough to feel guilty about over the course of a day (climate change, not caring about climate change, leaving our cats behind while we're at work), so ditch that clothes-have-feelings nonsense. It's completely weird and we all know this. That is the end of that.

Make sure you inherit everything

You can only acquire so much stuff of your own volition. That's why inheriting stuff is so important. It's basically like winning the stuff lottery and is never stressful or overwhelming at all. But you've got to plan ahead. My friend used to work at a company that handled a lot of estate planning. When a client died, he'd suddenly be fielding a bunch of calls from shady family members wanting to know how much they'd inherited and whether their sister did indeed get the ski chalet in Tahoe. The point is, these greedy fuckers were off their game. If you want to inherit shit, you've got to earn it, and you've got to lay the groundwork years in advance. Be the best daughter or son or sibling the world has ever seen. Don't like helping change your dad's poopy diapers or driving your aunt to her hospital appointments? Don't love reading Nicholas Sparks' latest novel aloud to your grandmother with failing eyesight? Kiss your inheritance goodbye. And enjoy looking at your grandmother's brass candlesticks you *specifically told grandma you wanted* sitting on your sister's mantel every time you go over to her house.

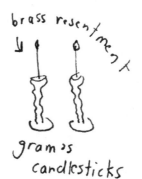

2.

The clutter blame game

"Some people look at a shelf stacked with coffee mugs and see only mugs. But people with serious disorganization problems might see each one as a unique item—a souvenir from Yellowstone or a treasured gift from Grandma."

—CERTIFIED
ORGANIZER COACH® [5]

5. From "A Clutter Too Deep for Mere Bins and Shelves," *New York Times*, January 1, 2008.

Oh fuck! Some of you (who have a serious disorganization problem) actually see items you own as having some kind of sentimental value. I'd like to meet all these well-adjusted sociopaths who don't give a shit about a treasured gift from their grandmother.

Let's be real: There's a lot of scaremongering about clutter's negative effect on our lives. We're all hyper-consumers and we're out of control and it's making us fat and miserable. This is what we're being told. Researchers at UCLA published a study called "Life at Home in the Twenty-First Century" that observed 32 families in Los Angeles and how they interacted with their material surroundings. Turns out, every time the women had to deal with their belongings, their stress level rose. Think about it. Just touching shit you own makes you stressed. The study is saying that unless you're planning to pull a Chris McCandless and burn all your belongings and move to Alaska and die in a bus, you're totally fucked. That's lifted verbatim from the conclusion of the study.

Here are more real things articles tell you about clutter. This kind of pearl clutching is usually reserved for local TV broadcasts about fraternity bros butt-chugging vodka.

- Clutter will give you germs. (You will kill your family with a clutter-related zombie virus because you didn't buy a pantry-organizing system.)

- In the above-referenced *New York Times* article, a doctor asserts, "If you can't find your sneakers, you aren't taking a walk." (You are going to develop health problems because you're an idiot and can no longer walk anywhere due to lack of footwear.)

- In addition, clutter will prevent you from shooting hoops with your son because you won't be able to find the basketball. (Don't worry, he'll be a meth-addict before you know it.)

- You may need cognitive behavioral therapy to help you tidy better. (You need professional help because you're so bad at life.)

- You're going to buy duplicate things because you can't find anything. (Like owning two lint rollers is going to bankrupt you.)

- And finally, clutter makes you fat. (Tidying makes you skinny.)

Many of these articles then go on to recommend a must-have book about decluttering (see earlier section: *Self-Help Books Are Bullshit*). Or a professional home organizer service. Or a therapist. Or a weight loss specialist. I read that one woman, whose garage was "a solid cube of clutter," cleaned it up and lost 50 pounds. Right. **Look, tidying your house will not make you drop a bunch of weight.** You will just have a tidy house for a while. Then it will be messy again. That's the real science.

45

with a lid!

box

The storage system conspiracy

You know who wants you to be tidy? The people at The Container Store. The CEO of Crate and Barrel. The accountant over at BINS BINS BINS. And why is that? Being neat is big business. The Clean Cartel wants you to feel ashamed of your mess. And thanks to capitalism, the only way to lose your shame is to buy things. Want to be a better person? Be more organized? Guess what? Buy all the things! But these things aren't really things. These are things to organize your things. Plastic storage bins. Wicker storage bins. Fabric-lined bins. Drawer dividers. But you can't buy just one of these things. You must buy the system. See how that works? A simple basket isn't enough to organize you. Now you must purchase a storage system—for your bedroom, your office, your pantry. . . .

These are actual things you can buy at a store:

- Crystal cosmetic stacking organizer

- Premium stacking shoe bin

- Box with lid

Hundreds of dollars later, you've got more debt on your credit card and you've still got shit lying everywhere. Why is that? Mess cannot be contained. It wants to be FREE. Embrace it. Save your money and go on a road trip to Nashville or to see the world's biggest nickel (that's in Sudbury, fools). Buy a flight to South Beach or Edmonton. Buy something that is as pointless as a closet organizer but way more fun. A waist trainer? A wine club subscription? Step outside the organizing insanity and see it for what it really is.

I'll let you in on a little secret. You can put your stuff anywhere. It doesn't have to be placed in a corporate-sanctioned bin. In fact, if you've been paying attention, you'll have already realized that you don't have to place your stuff anywhere. But if you must, for example, place a heap of things into a contained space, I recommend a laundry basket. These open-topped beauties are durable, breathable, and easy to lift. Move your shit from place to place with ease. Or let it sit there. Whatever.

let's use logic to determine whether
you need a storage system

1. Do you have a lot of extra money?
2. Have you ever been to Italy?

If you answered "no" to either question, you don't need a storage system. Here's why:

If you have extra money, and you haven't been to Italy, do that. It's amazing. Sure, Venice is expensive and the Amalfi Coast is touristy, but it's beautiful and the wine is cheap and do you want to die without having Instagrammed a wheel of Italian cheese in Florence? Also when you get older, long plane flights become an issue. Sitting for that long is a bitch. Go now. While you still have time and healthy knees.

If you don't have extra money, but you have been to Italy, congrats on your trip, but you can't afford a storage system. That's an easy one.

If you have extra money and you've also been to Italy already, congrats on being part of the one percent. You probably also have a cleaning lady, so why are you even reading this?

CLUTTER REALITY CHECK: If you're not having sex, it's not because you're messy

Just like having a baby will not fix your troubled relationship with your husband or wife, cleaning your house will not enable you to suddenly have better/more frequent/more sex. Books that promise you this are lying to you. If you bought this book looking for sex advice, you have more problems than I can help you with. *Oh, you haven't had sex with your partner in over a year? Organize your closet and see what happens! Nothing will make you want to fuck more than having all your T-shirts neatly folded in a drawer.* Here's a secret: If you want to have sex, just go fuck someone. On a pile of laundry, in a hot tub, in a public bathroom, on a dumpster (or in the dumpster, feel me?), whatever. University and college students are very good at this— eighteen-year-olds will literally have sex with anyone anywhere. If teenagers can find the time and energy to finger each other quietly under the blankets while watching TV in your living room, you can find time to have sex too. If you're not having sex, the reason isn't your messy house. In fact, if you're not having sex, it may be because your house isn't messy enough.

Here's a visualization exercise I'd like you to try: Think of a friend, celebrity, or politician (we know you're thinking of Trudeau, you dirty Canucks) that you'd like to fuck. Now think about whether your house is clean. Un-fucking-related, right? So chin up and go get what's yours. Booze helps. Here are some other fixes for your shitty sex life: Is your Tinder profile up to date? Sex (or at least numerous dick pics) is just a swipe away. Are there dogs and cats and children in your bed? Have sex on the floor. Do you need sexier lingerie? Rip the crotch out of some panties. Do you need a wax? Fucking get it done. (Although bush is back these days. So find someone that loves a giant bush and bone them.) Remember: The only books that can fix your sex drive are books by V. C. Andrews. And only if all the pages are there.

3.

Leave your sh*t all over the house

"A house is just a pile of stuff with a cover on it. . . . That's what your house is, a place to keep your stuff while you go out and get more stuff."

—GEORGE CARLIN

If you decide that it's okay for your closet to be cluttered but then freak the fuck out about your messy desk, you're failing at being messy. You have to take a holistic approach to leaving your shit everywhere. You have to own it. Then buy more stuff and own that, too.

HOME OFFICE: The messier the desk, the more creative the mind

↑ messy desk ↗

If you're like me, your desk is your sanctuary. It's where you get things done or avoid getting things done. These days, depending on your job, your desk probably consists of your laptop and maybe a coaster for your coffee mug. Perhaps you need a notebook and a few pens. Maybe also your phone. And a small, chic lamp with a nice lamp shade so you can see what you're doing. Likely you need a bright houseplant or succulent or two for inspiration. A few books for reference. Some old bills you've been meaning to pay online. A funny snow globe from Vegas. The latest *London Review of Books* and *Us Weekly* you've been meaning to read.[6] Aren't Andrew O'Hagan and Vanderpump Rules amazing? Maybe a few boxes and baskets from the organization section of your local big box store, filled with papers, photos, cords, a purple stapler, some batteries. An old coffee mug from yesterday. Right. So your desk is a fucking mess. You know who had a messy desk? Einstein. It even had a cookie jar. You know who had a tidy desk? Mussolini. But

....

6. I once met the then-editor of *Us Weekly* in a bar in Manhattan. I asked him many questions about whether or not he thought Beyoncé's pregnancy belly was real. We came to no definitive conclusion, but it definitely wasn't real.

Einstein wasn't just an anomaly—the benefits of a messy desk are supported by scientific research.

ideas & hair

Einstein

A messy desk is actually better for creativity, according to all the scientists you went to school with who are now making more money than you. Researchers at the University of Minnesota (see page 13) and Northwestern came up with similar results: When test subjects were placed in a clean room, they showed more conventional thinking when it came to creative uses for ping-pong balls. (Yup, beer pong.) The people in the messy room? They came up with crazier uses for ping-pong balls (especially if they'd been to a sex show in Amsterdam).

Being in a messy environment means you're more fucking interesting. It means your brain is fired up and making weird connections. It means you're less likely to stick with conventional ideas. Example: My hairdresser and I were talking about an upcoming snowstorm and he said something like, "It really makes you wonder." Wonder what? I asked. "Who controls the weather," he said. He thinks the government controls the weather. He was from Florida, though, so maybe it's not all his fault. But I bet his desk is fucking messy as hell.

super creative
brain

So guess what? All those books telling you to declutter for peace of mind are actually making you more boring. Cleanliness encourages you to live a mundane lifestyle. A predictable lifestyle. One with beige walls and floors and ceilings that keeps you enclosed in its little cube of boredom as you advance slowly toward mediocrity and death. But escape is easy enough. And if your desk is already messy—congratulations! You're probably one step away from writing the next *SCUM Manifesto* or inventing an app to cure loneliness.

Join the messy desk revolution and start thinking about weird things. Put a GoPro on your carp. Make a mug of that flowered herbal tea you brought back from Bhutan (*the first nation in the world to ban plastic bags,* you'll tell anyone who'll listen). Carve your lover's initials into your desk or forearm. Add your name to the list of awesome people who contribute to society and whose desks are (or were) messy as shit and who don't belong to the cult of keeping things clean: Anne Sexton, Charlotte Perkins Gilman, Mark Zuckerberg, Steve Jobs. Hell, Sylvia Plath wrote on a typewriter outdoors, according to a photo I saw on the internet. Ditch the desk altogether and just find a field full of ants somewhere and get inspired.

BATHROOM: Indoor plumbing is a privilege. Don't fu*k with it.

Take a walk over to your bathroom. Whether it's a shitty rental bathroom in Astoria or a nice cabin bathroom in Muskoka, I bet it's a tiny bit of a disaster. The mirror has spots on it. The hand towel has mascara on it. And maybe your moisturizer with SPF 45 is still sitting on the counter from earlier this morning. Along with your pants from last night. And your shoes. Maybe there are four or five hair ties scattered around, helpfully. There's probably also a wicker storage basket or two nearby, overflowing with various products that make you look amazing. I mean, how could you not? Especially after those Korean beauty products hit the market in a real way and you went insane like the rest of us for sheet masks and essences and serums and snail mucus. The Tidy Club suggests putting everything away after you use it. If I did that, I wouldn't be able to find anything and would then just have to buy more things, which wouldn't be so bad. It's all probably the same cream made in the same factory in China and packaged in different bottles, but that's not for us to judge. Anyway, leave all your products out where you can see them. If you're one of those people that only uses, like, lip balm and Vaseline and a bar of soap for your beauty routine, congratulations—but your bathroom is still messy, I'm betting.

Besides, who gives a shit about being tidy in your bathroom? Only people you like or who you're fucking will see it. (Or the plumber, maybe, sometimes.) I say just be fucking grateful for having a bathroom at all. One hundred years ago, you'd be pooping outside and worrying about sweeping the outhouse floor, probably.

More than 2.6 billion people do not have indoor plumbing—including more than 1.5 million Americans. It's a wonderful thing, whether or not there's clutter or the décor is exactly as you want it. My dad grew up in England after the war, and for years he bathed in an old copper tub in the front room, like some kind of adorable Victorian. That was just one generation ago. So spare me your sob story about how all the bathrooms you've pinned on Pinterest are unattainable. You want cedar benches and marble countertops? Copper hardware? Rainforest shower? All-white spa towels? Heated floors? Hotel-level cleanliness? You probably also wanted to run a B&B in Goa after your life-changing trip to India 10 years ago, and wish your stomach were flatter, too.

Check yourself for a moment, you ungrateful

wench. Think about how great it is to have your poop quickly funneled away from your house with the touch of a handle. Acknowledge that it is very cool not to have to schlep your poop outside in a bucket. Now, once you've appreciated how good you have it, rummage around in one of those wicker storage baskets, pull out a sheet mask (snail mucus ones are the best), and slap that thing on your face. Make sure to take a selfie, because those things are creepy as hell.

KITCHEN: You have to eat to live, and that's going to make a mess

unwashed everything

I don't actually use my kitchen because I live within a block of 47 restaurants and I have a lot of money to spend on eating out because writers are wealthy people. I use my stove for storage. It's filled with a bunch of diner mugs. My fridge is a bar fridge. Or what Europeans call a fridge because everything over there is one-third the size of American things. It's filled with mixers for my rye and vodka and rum. I know from social media and Pinterest that a lot of you have nice-looking kitchens. You use them to store and make food. I've also learned from accidentally clicking on baking blogs while browsing for porn ("Sweaty Betty in the Kitchen" is a misleading name, no?) that baking can be messy. Why bother trying to clean that shit up? You probably know how to make five or six things maximum, so you're going to use the same ingredients over and over. What's the point of cleaning up a mess if you're just going to make another mess a few hours later?

For example, baking a "naked cake" involves flour, sugar, baking soda, cake mix, chocolate chips, salmon, fresh-cut flowers, plus a bunch of bowls, mixers, and spoons, probably. You have that after dinner and then it's time for coffee and the sugar is already out. Yes, being messy means being more efficient.

thing in your fridge ↙

old tomato?

Quantity is also key for every kitchen space. The more utensils and ingredients the better. You should definitely own as many appliances as you can. Donut makers. Deep fryers. Vegetable spiralizers. Coffee grinders. Ice cream makers. Slow cookers. Knife sharpeners. Automatic can openers. When you're done cooking, tell your kitchen *thank you for your service.* Or better yet, tell your kitchen to chill the fuck out and then throw your dirty dishes out the window. I had a friend that used to do this in university. It works best with a lot of snow. And no people, obviously. Then, when everything melts in the spring, you've got a yard full of pans and dishes and it's basically a Picasso sculpture from his Surrealist period (thanks MoMA) or some hippie's front yard art installation in Santa Fe.

PANTRY: Buy now, eat later

You need more cans of soup. Armageddon hasn't happened yet, but it will soon. The dollar could tank. The banks could not be big enough and fail. The big one could hit California. Your Internet could go out for a few hours. Buy that shit in bulk and stock up. Stockpiling food is a real thing you should do—it isn't just for insane militiamen anymore. The more food, the better. Who knows how long the radiation could last. Don't have a pantry? Use the garage or a spare bedroom. Nothing is more fun at a dinner party than taking your guests on a tour of your 40 cases of Amy's Organic Lentil Soup and economy-size Clinique moisturizer. Side note: When Armageddon hits, say goodbye to your vegan or gluten-free diet. You're going to be eating shit that's more upsetting to your stomach than a few wheat molecules.

BEDROOM: A fu*king glorious mess

My grandmother used to starch and iron her bed linens. She also raised four kids and had a job at the post office. This isn't to shame you about why your bedroom looks like shit but to demonstrate how far we've come as a society. My grandmother did that because she lived in a small

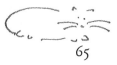

town of 400 people in the 1940s, and if she *didn't* do that shit, word would get out and the other ladies around town would disapprove. Or maybe they'd have been like, *that's a great idea*, and the patriarchy would have fallen years ago. But here we are and the only starched linens you'll ever see are in a hotel. And that's the way it should be. You know why? People at the hotel are paid a (hopefully) living wage to starch those sheets. You and me, my friend, have other things to do. Our bedrooms are for sleeping, napping, laptop watching, cookie eating, dressing and undressing, sex-having, snoring, etc. Bedrooms should be piled high with clothing piles. The duvet should be on the floor. The sheets all tangled and covered in ink stains from your incessant journaling. The blinds askew because they're those venetian blinds that only go up on one side and now the cord is all tangled and you haven't had time to fix them. There's a dog bed in the corner even through your dog sleeps on your bed most nights. Some condom wrappers on the floor. A few clothing items hanging from the doorknob. A fucking glorious mess. Pat yourself on the back.

Our grandmothers would be horrified at the state of our bedrooms. And also a little jealous. Who knows what they would have done with all that free time?

CLOSET: Does it have a door? Shut it.

rumpled pineapple
sweater

My husband and I share a small one-bedroom apartment. In this apartment is one closet. Not one bedroom closet. One closet total. We both hang our clothes in it. We share it. It's full, and it's fine. We don't need systems. We don't need special hangers. We have clothing, we hang it up. Or we leave it on the floor. End of story. If no more shit can fit, we get rid of some of it. (I donate his clothing when he's at work.) This is how you can effectively deal with your closet. By not trying so hard.

Go stand in front of your closet. Do it now. You'll never get the most out of this book if you don't do all the exercises. Now look at your closet. Are the clothes organized from lightest to darkest? From summer clothing to winter? What about by color? Probably not, right? Are the clothes a jumbled mess on the floor? A few things hung up inside-out or with cat hair on them? Do you see a few items in there you don't really wear anymore? Super. You're a fucking failure. Go jump out the window because you're literally never going to have sex again. Kidding.

You are in the majority of closet owners. But you're not happy. Why is that? Because society

says your closet should be organized and your life will be changed for the better once you do that. For example, HGTV recommends scheduling an hour out of your week to declutter your closet. What the living fuck. I love you, 5-hour HGTV marathons, but don't tell me what to do. What are we left with? A closet that's messy and the guilt that comes from various sources telling us to tidy it. *Closet solutions. Closet systems. Just an hour a day!* Why is no one calling bullshit? Being told your closet isn't up to snuff is irritating. You have permission to have a messy closet. That's why most closets have doors. Is the door closed? Great. On to the next chapter, where we'll look at how to handle specific items within your messy home.

4.

Dealing with the actual sh*t in your house

"Buying is a profound pleasure."
—SIMONE DE BEAUVOIR

Every room gets messy differently. That's why when you're ignoring clutter and mess, it's good to learn how to do it by category. Your clothing heaps deserve just as little attention as your knickknacks and paddywhacks. Whether it's clutter from too many children or simply from your fantastic collection of plants that are somehow not dead yet, we'll take a look at how to ensure everything you own is piled in heaps and in multiples of two so you can get on with your life. Sound joyful? That's because it is.

CLOTHES: Don't fold them or they'll wrinkle

Retailers pay employees to hand-steam T-shirts and fold them into little origami swans to make you want to buy them. Fine. I'll buy another 40-dollar "tissue" tee from J. Crew which I'll immediately get caught on a nail. But don't bring that mentality home with you. Once you've bought something, take it out of the bag, rip the tags off it, and wear it immediately for the rest of the day and preferably also as pajamas that night. The key to wearing it in perfectly is to get it stained as quickly as possible. For me, it's usually coffee or errant BB cream that does the trick. Once it's broken in, you can relax. Take it off, leave it on the floor, step on it and around it. Let it marinate there until next time you need it. And rest assured it will be 100 percent broken in and cool looking. Oh, this T-shirt I wore to your birthday party? Yeah, thanks, I'm wearing it to show I 100 percent do not give a fuck what anyone thinks of me, which is a fashion choice of sorts, which perpetuates the idea that rumpled = cool. Which it does. So stop being a square and worrying about folding your jeans. You don't have time for that, and you're not in the military where you can't even wear jeans anyway. Next.

LOUNGEWEAR: It's all you should wear

My coworker wore black yoga pants to work one day, and her husband was like, "So you've given up?" Joke is on him. Yoga pants are comfortable, and you should own 40 pairs even if you don't yoga. Feel free to also own sexy shit, but let's all acknowledge that most of us go to bed in dick-shriveling sweatpants. Realizing that your clothes should only consist of loungewear is part of growing up. When you move in with your first boyfriend, you're like, *Must invest in a bunch of lace nighties and shave my vag.* Every night you're lounging in Victoria's Secret line of sex-worker-inspired bras. Your only fee is the D, get me? Then 10 years later you're investing in a robe made of 1,000 rabbit furs and socks lined with sheep faces and you've never been more comfortable. You've realized that going to sleep and being comfortable are your rights as a human being. You've stopped dressing for anyone else. Plus, loungewear still looks amazing when it's wrinkled, and you wash it maybe every two weeks, tops.

Know this: Lingerie is just a big conspiracy. Sure, it's fun to wear, and fun to buy, and you should own a shit ton of it. But it's for special

occasions—not every day. Have you ever tried hanging around in a silk nightgown for example? They're slippery as fuck. And when you spill wine on them, they stain really easily. Have you ever had a lace front-wedgie? Not fucking pleasant. Don't believe anyone who tells you they wear sexy lingerie to bed every night. Especially if they live in a cold climate. Literally everyone in Saskatchewan wears an entire fleece outfit made by Roots to bed every night from October through May because it's the best. So stock up. Jogging pants. Hoodies. Onesies. Socks. T-shirts. Golden Rule: If it's elastic, it feels fantastic.

PURSE: 90 items or fewer

If you have to leave the country and start over from scratch in Costa Rica (where all criminals go to party), your purse should already contain everything you need. Passport. Fresh panties. Aspirin. Lipstick. Selfie stick. Flask. Credit card. Tiny snub-nosed handgun like from the movies. Burner cell phone.

That's why you should always purchase the biggest purse you can carry. Here's a good purse test: Can it fit a bottle of wine? No? Move on. Yes? Buy it. Then fill it with everything you need and never empty it or clean it. Those 40 pennies in the bottom will work themselves out somehow. The KonMari Method, on the other hand, advocates emptying your purse every night, folding it, and thanking it for its service. Can you fucking imagine? I'm telling you right now that's the road to insanity. Your one-night stand

purse

is definitely going to write you into his next screenplay if you do that shit.

Your purse is big and full of stuff because you need stuff throughout your day. No one likes the evenings they're forced to use a fucking clutch. A clutch fits half a tampon and half your phone. Pointless. And later, when you want to check your abacus or tag an overpass, you won't have the right tools. So embrace your giant purse. And remember, when you're stuck on the Q train because the FDNY is rescuing homeless kittens from the tracks, your airline almonds, flashlight, bolt cutters, and cat food will come in handy while you're Snapchatting your followers about the delay.

SHOES: Keep them

Accumulating as many shoes as possible is an acceptable goal in life. I still have shoes from 1999—Spice Girls-era high-heeled sport sandals. And don't worry about spraying protector

on them—that shit is a scam run by the shoe stores. If you own suede boots, don't wear them in the rain. That's your real protection.

An acceptable number of shoes to own is 45 pairs—or one pair for each year of your life. You probably already own at least three pairs of Havaianas, some running shoes, and some peach satin bridesmaid heels your friend was like, "you can dye them black!" That friend is divorced now, but you should keep the shoes. Keep all the shoes. Fuck the shoe trees and shoeboxes. Leave them everywhere.

Your partner leaves his/her shoes in the living room. They're size 11, so it's not like they're hard to miss. You:

A. sweep them to the side of the room with your foot.

B. sigh loudly, pick up the shoes, and put them away where they belong. Remember when you were seventeen and thought you'd take the bus out to LA and become an actress? It was fun when life held possibilities, wasn't it?

C. exclaim, "Something to tidy!" and enthusiastically place Clippy and Cloppy away on their shelf, while thanking them for giving you something to do now that the kids are in college and that morning bottle of wine is finished.

D. do nothing.

1,000 pairs of shoes

Let me enlighten you. The only options that will allow you to retain your sanity are A or D. Being mad about clutter is a waste of time. Being happy about it is pretty weird. Acceptance is key. Either casually deal with the tripping hazard, or don't. On your deathbed, will you be like, "Super glad I always got mad about shoes"? Or, will you remember the feeling of freedom as you lived life free of society's restrictions?

KIDS: The very definition of messy

I have a few friends on social media who have five or more children. Not in a sad oppressed cult way (totally in a cult way) but because they enjoy kids and love them and want to have a big family. At least that's what I assume, because they seem happy, and social media is never wrong. I also have friends with one small baby. If you walked into the houses of either of these families, there would be kid mess, probably. I avoid houses with children under six in them because visiting a house with tiny kids is super stressful. You think you're in for some gossip and possibly a discussion about the World Bank and whether Thomas Piketty's *Capital in the Twenty-First Century* was the book of the decade and whether they agree that carrots are the new kale, but instead there are strollers and play mats and pumping supplies and burp cloths and the detritus of children everywhere. They literally haven't read *TMZ* in months, and all you end up doing is staring at their kid and commenting on how cute they are and how big they're getting before taking off after an hour. (Let's face it, babies that aren't your own are boring. They do not "like" bubbles and Raffi at two months old, despite what your monthly updates would have your followers believe. They are blobs without preferences. Give me a six-year-old, obsessed with dinosaurs and robots and wearing his pants on his head any day. That shit is weird and hilarious.)

Anyway. Parents: It has never been more important to remember you'll be dead soon. Because know this: Your house will not be tidy if there are children in it. Isn't knowing that more than enough reason to give this not-giving-a-fuck thing a shot? You can have the tidiest house in the world but your teenager's rank, semeny bedroom is going to make you cry. So your option is 18 or more years of being stressed about kid mess or just dealing with it. You probably love them and hopefully mostly like them and aren't consumed by thoughts of the path not taken or your lost vagina. It used to be so tight, right? So lighten up. And learn something from the little ones. Are they ever concerned with mess? Probably not. Kids don't give a fuck about anything, as you well know. When do we lose that ability to just enjoy our environment as-is? Go bedazzle some denim or cover the driveway in sidewalk chalk or fingerpaint a wall or something. Being an adult is hard. Being a parent is even harder. You can only control so much. Concentrate on the important stuff—like what kindergarten program gives your three-year-old the best shot at getting into Harvard.

cat pile

Meow

Secret mouse

CATS: Buy more cats

Cat people have a bad reputation. The more cats you have, the more likely you are to be insane or acquire *Toxoplasma gondii*, which rewires your neurons to make you more or less outgoing, depending on your gender. Some people think cats are shady, and they'd be right, but if you don't "get" cats you should just go buy a hundred gerbils. But there's a reason people who like cats seem to end up with a million of them. Because they are fluffy and quiet and everyone likes quiet, fluffy things. You should always have a few more cats than seems reasonable. Golden Rule: If you like cats, you should have a bunch.

DOGS: Ditto

In order to have a bunch of dogs, you should probably live in the country, otherwise it's kind of mean. You just look like a selfish dick when you walk your greyhound around Tribeca. I know you're rich and have a big apartment—but it's not that big. Get a fucking house in the country, so that thing can run around properly. Dogs are also great because they come with a lot of accessories. Your dog should own at least 10 sweaters, a few coats, and a bunch of cute little plastic shoes to protect its feet from salt and snow. There's no excuse not to have dog clutter.

If your dog doesn't own a whole bunch of adorable dog accessories, you're basically not taking care of it properly. If you live in the country and have a real dog, however, you're excused from buying cutesy accessories. Just give it a horse leg or turkey jaw or whatever country dogs eat and let it run around and get sprayed by a skunk or attacked by a porcupine and enjoy country life.

BOOKS: Buy them, pile them

If you're a book person, you already inherently know this: Books are important, and it's okay to own thousands of them and never get rid of them. This requires bookshelves, possibly. But the great thing about books is they're imminently stackable. Your bedside table is the obvious place to start. When that's full, try the floor next to it. Windowsills. Chairs. Obviously a few books go in the bathroom for when your phone battery is dead. Work-related books by your desk. Cookbooks in the kitchen. Coffee table books on the

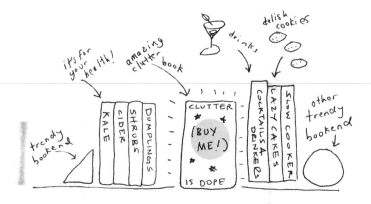

it's for your health!

amazing clutter book

drinks

delish cookies

trendy bookend

KALE
CIDER
SHRUBS
DUMPLINGS

CLUTTER
★ ★
(BUY ME!)
★
✿
IS DOPE

COCKTAILS & DRINKS
CRAZY CAKES
SLOW COOKER

other trendy bookend

coffee table. Old, weird books in the attic or garage. Acquiring more books is important, too. Any trip to a place that sells books of any kind requires you to purchase one. You could be eight months behind on your rent, and if you don't buy a book at a used bookstore, you're basically a bad person who doesn't love to read.

Acceptable reasons to downsize your collection are: you're hiking the Pacific Crest Trail and you need to rip and discard the pages you've already read to lighten your backpack.

Books are not clutter, no matter what some

book about getting organized may tell you. Literally no one has ever walked into a library and been like, *What a fucking mess*. Also, it's difficult to judge people properly if they don't own any books. Oh, your favorite author is David Foster Wallace? Congrats on reading one book in university. You recommend *The Alchemist*? Can you also share with me some inspirational sayings from your Instagram stream? You loved *The Millionaire Next Door*? Nice work on your business degree and hope the real estate thing works out for you. You prefer *The Story of O* to *Fifty Shades of Grey*? Your friends think you're pretentious. Subscribe to *People*? You love Fireball shots and are actually pretty fun at parties. Your favorite book is *Moby Dick*? Go fuck yourself. See how it works? Plus, if you go to a new friend's house for the first time and they have *no* books, you can basically turn the fuck around and never talk to them again. So keep those books where we can see them.

5.

Leave some sh*t outside and in cyberspace

"You might be a redneck if . . . you didn't put pink plastic flamingos in your front yard as a joke."

—JEFF FOXWORTHY

Mess isn't just for houses anymore. Step outside and embrace the beauty of messy yards, cars, and inboxes. If you're not messy in every area of your life, you're missing an opportunity to be lazier.

YARD: Keep plastic and broken stuff hidden behind the house. If there's room.

When I was in my early twenties, I worked as a door-to-door fundraiser for various charities. It sounds a bit shady (definitely was) but the organizations agreed to contract us as fundraisers and we went out and raised money for them. Some donors got bent out of shape when they found out we were getting paid, but we were happy for the work. We were all basically unemployable: kids with no job experience, random Europeans working illegally for extra cash, or people for whom a regular office wasn't a good fit. Like my coworker who had done time for attempted murder. I got to see a lot of doorbells, quirky door knockers, and lawn ornaments, and meet lots of nice ladies who'd invite me in for lemonade. The point of all this is that in Chatham, Ontario, there were about 20 houses on one street that had cement geese out front. Geese that the homeowners had painted and dressed up in bonnets or straw hats. This is the correct way to decorate your yard. By filling it with random shit.

If you're stressed about your garden not being a perfect Zen paradise with white rocks and mini Bonsai artfully arranged, I'm sorry about your feelings. But your yard has a purpose, and that's for storage and tacky decorations. So hoist up those unfunny "Attention: Spoiled Grandchildren Ahead" signs and stick them proudly in your garden. Salute the remnants of that sandbox that seemed like a good idea until the raccoons started shitting in it. Let a family of beavers nest in the rusted shell of your old Honda. Paint your garage with your favorite team logo, you utter cock. Let everything run amok.

HOLIDAY DECORATIONS: Yes

Embracing clutter around the holidays can be tough, depending on whether you're excellent at clutter or whether it still stresses you out. The prospect of adding plastic skeletons, paper turkeys, menorahs, Easter bunnies, and inflatable Santas to your décor can feel a bit overwhelming. The key is to go all out. I have an aunt who collects Christmas trees. She literally owns 500 trees and puts them up every holiday season and then takes them down again in January. People go similarly nuts for Halloween. My friend in South Carolina turns her front yard into a haunted cemetery, complete with animatronic witches and plastic severed body parts. Our capitalist overlords know this, and that's why you can buy a turkey-themed literally anything

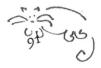

around Thanksgiving. Turkey ashtray? Sure. Turkey-scented candle? Yes. Turkey-skin martini? Yum. Turkey onesie? Snuggle me! Paper flag banner from Etsy that says "Merry and Bright"? Hang that shit up because it's almost Christmas. Leave it up all year.

Forget your chic, modern holiday with your white ceramic decorations. Get those boxes out from storage, make your own decorations, head to the Dollar Store, or whatever you need to do. Holidays aren't about sleek, empty, magazine-ready space. Holidays are tacky as fuck and definitely cluttered. Enjoy it. And remember to enjoy the seasonal booze: Absolut Mistletoe and Captain Morgan's Leftist Labor Day Rum. Embrace the festive spirit.

find your h₀liday clutter style here:

1. If you could pick one holiday and only celebrate that one for the rest of your life, what
would it be?

   A. my birthday

   B. Administrative Professionals Day

   C. Indigenous Peoples' Day

2. You're at a big box store. What's your
splurge?

   A. a 16-pack of sponges

   B. a curved flat-screen television and imitation
      crab dip

   C. you don't shop at big box stores. You prefer
      Etsy or local craft markets you can bike to.

3. Venice is sinking. What action do you take to help?

   A. find a designated, approved charity like the Red Cross and donate as much as you can afford.

   B. find out what people need on the ground and organize a shopping expedition to fill those needs: bleach, mops, cleaning supplies, etc. Also find out if you can order some discount blown Venetian glass, pasta, and Pecorino from the flooded shops while you're at it.

   C. volunteer for Habitat For Humanity and carpool over to Italy to help rebuild.

Your holiday style:

Mostly As: **Martha Stewart's responsible niece.** You're practical and organized. Maybe you bought this book because you know that and want to learn a bit more about letting go. You like to spend money if it's on something you need. You're not really into kitschy stuff. You like to pour your orange juice at night and put plastic wrap over it so you can have it chilled and fresh in the morning.

Mostly Bs: Ho-ho-holiday elf. You're a hoe for the holidays (any holiday) and you love buying stuff and making people happy. You're the friend that bakes cookies for holiday parties and hand-paints ornaments with inside jokes on them for presents. #MiamiGoals #LeBron is an actual thing you wrote on your ornament gifts this year for all your sorority girls from FSU or something. Not sure if that makes sense, because in Canada, where I'm from, we barely have basketball, let alone sororities. The point is, you run the holidays. Congrats.

Mostly Cs: Low-key holiday tofu loaf. You're not into consumerism, or holidays, so your house is lame and no one likes visiting you. You celebrate the least among us. Those who aren't so fortunate. You feel guilty about enjoying holidays when others have so little. This is admirable, I guess, but if you're looking for a break from saving the world, it's okay to reach for a bottle of whiskey and some glitter.

CARS: Out the window or into the backseat

When I worked at Cedar Point in Ohio, a coworker asked if I wanted to help her clean her car. I said yes because that's the kind of thing you do when you're twenty and it's your day off. The mess in her car was epic. It was the most inspiring thing I've ever seen. She was particularly fond of White Castle, and there were dozens of those tiny burger containers in the backseat. She also had, like, five of those round gum containers designed to fit in the cupholder of your car, but because the cupholder was full of other stuff, they were just lying on the floor of the passenger seat. If she'd had an ant farm and five stillborn babies in the trunk, I would not have been surprised. Then she cleaned her car by opening all the doors and scooping the mess out onto the pavement and driving her car to a new parking space. The point of this is that she was a borderline sociopath but she was doing "having a car" correctly. I learned a lot from her, including how to shoplift.

is there junk in the
trunk of your weird
car?

Cars are mobile storage palaces. Thinking of paying for a storage unit? Don't be a sucker. Extra cowboy hats? Car. Stuff to take to the Goodwill or Amity? Trunk. Stilettos and McDonald's fries left over from your club night when your friend balled that NBA player in his hotel? Backseat. Dog blankets, car seats, emergency shovel, binder full of CDs featuring TLC and Blackstreet (or Lifehouse and Sugar Ray, depending on your preference)—good for you. When you're stranded overnight in a snowstorm on the Trans-Canada highway (Canada's Route 66, except still very useful and a bit colder), heading from Ottawa to Winnipeg, you aren't going to be relieved that your car is nice and tidy. You're going to be stoked that you've got a box of Timbits in the backseat, a SONY Discman, a case of beer, a snowblower, and a book about Confederation to put you to sleep. Basically, your car should always contain everything you need in the event of the Apocalypse.

DIGITAL: Leave a big digital footprint

all your selfies

online 4-ever

Anti-clutter books or science will tell you words are stressful but they should all fuck off (and those do-gooder authors should embrace the irony of writing a whole book or peer-reviewed journal article about how words are stressful). *Too many words and your brain can't concentrate. Too much multi-tasking and you'll forget stuff.* Guess what? If you forget things you can look them up online. Just as calculators mean we don't have to remember how to multiply anymore, so the Internet releases us from the responsibility of ever remembering anything again. Yet think pieces about the danger of digital clutter are everywhere. *Digital clutter is all up in your head, fucking up your day-to-day life with notifications and dings and voicemail messages from your mom.* This is normal. We are all now cyborgs from a dystopian novel about mind control and you shouldn't care, because smartphones and the Internet are amazing. I can order cat food online and have it delivered to my door two hours later. My cats love the Internet. Obviously I'll be the first to die if there's some kind of robot uprising or general systems failure and I have to leave the house in January to trade cigarettes on the black market for food. But until then, let's agree our lives have been easier since Al Gore invented the Internet.

Despite this, you can't read *Good Housekeeping* or listen to a *Slate* podcast without some nut telling you all about the joys of a digital detox. *Oh, I lived in a tree for a month and now my mind is clear and I can focus on my shuffleboard game and designing this arrow logo for my house-made condiments line.* By all means take a digital detox for a week, if you can hack it, or go live out in Slab City, California—an off-the-grid community of squatters in the desert with no electricity or water or anything.

But generally we're all living in smart homes and connected cars now and we have to find a way to deal with it. Emails are stressful? Boo hoo. Guess what? They aren't. Email is fast and convenient and literally the easiest thing in the world to manage. You should have as many email addresses as possible. Keep your Yahoo, AOL, or Hotmail one for nostalgia and your Gmail or .me for your real business and a few extras for catfishing and Ashley Madison purposes.

Try thinking about it this way: Emails are

amazing, and every time you receive one, try to be grateful for how much collective intelligence and energy went into creating the mechanisms enabling you to receive 4,000 emails from LinkedIn every day. You like Crate and Barrel? They want to be friends with you too! Can't remember which of the Great Lakes is the deepest? Look that shit up! Open 12 tabs and switch between them for hours. Consume as much information as you can. Read about world news and celebrities and watch clips of important events. Comment on various articles and share opinions with friends. Get involved in some public shaming when someone posts or writes something you don't like. Fill your brain with information and distraction and communication. We've never, in the history of the world, had access to so much information. Libraries don't count, sorry.

Then, rest comfortably, knowing that if you ever get famous, some screenwriter in 2087 is going to buy access to all your online searches and social media accounts to help them research your biopic. That Chopin had a foot fetish is something we might know if there had been Google back in the early 1800s. From this point forward, everyone in the future will have the ability to know everything about us. Forget your memoir that carefully examines your inner life, using the metaphor of a wisteria that grew in your front yard that was planted by your grandmother. Years from now, voyeurs will scroll through your search history and emails and photos and know the real, unfiltered you. Now, if that isn't a relaxing thought, you're not doing life correctly.

delete?

save all the emails!

How many unread emails do you have in your inbox?

A. more than 2,000

B. none

If you answered A: you subscribe to a lot of mailing lists and don't answer or open all your emails in what society deems to be a timely fashion. Accept that you're never going to answer all the email you want in an appropriate amount of time and with the appropriate level of effort. Lots of emails means you're popular, so you definitely won't end up alone— you've got Madewell and Sephora for friends!

If you answered B: you answer or delete or sort all your emails. Good for you, I guess. You probably could have skipped reading this section, but you seem like the kind of person who likes to be thorough.

6.

Cherish your stuff but do not hoard

"And happy always was it for that son, whose father for his hoarding went to hell."
—WILLIAM SHAKESPEARE

While other books endorse a militant attitude toward cleanliness (those authors would prefer it if you lived in a hypo-allergenic white box and owned four pairs of white leotards), messiness is a fine art. Done right, it's beautiful. Once you've tipped the scales from messiness and clutter into hoarding, though, you've got a problem. Look, your dad isn't going to hell if he's a hoarder, and neither will you, probably. But hoarding is a serious thing that could signify some bigger issues and also get you on television. Hopefully while you're still alive, but maybe after you're dead.

Have you heard of the Collyer brothers? They're the famous reclusive brothers who accumulated over 140 tons of stuff in their Harlem brownstone. One brother was crushed to death under a mountain of debris and the other starved after his brother died. Here are some things that were removed from the house after their bodies were discovered:

- pickled human organs

- 25,000 books

- eight live cats

- a car

- fourteen pianos

- "old food"

Hopefully, from the above list you've intuited the difference between clutter and hoarding.

Hoarding is reality-television level insanity. Hoarding is when you buy 40 egg timers at the dollar store and leave them in the bag with the

tags on, then put the bag on your couch, and repeat until no one can find your body when you die because it's under a pile of egg timers and *New Yorker* mags from 2005 and the bodies of your parakeets and the instruction manual to your Roomba that died from frustration. Actually, fuck it. That house sounds awesome. There are probably only a few things you should ever throw away. Things like:

- food that's past its expiration date

- used cat litter

- empty bottles of shampoo or conditioner

- plants that have died

- pickled organs

- anything that was alive and is now dead

1. Are there any rotting fruits in your living room?

   A. yes, but they are the pumpkins I bought and meant to carve for Halloween. Now I'm definitely going to make them into pumpkin bread.

   B. yes, but they are the pumpkins I carved for Halloween, so they're more folk art than rotting fruit.

   C. yes, but my rotten fruit is in the fruit bowl where it belongs.

2. How many cats do you own?

   A. 10

   B. I'm not exactly sure, some are in the house in Vail and some are in the apartment in Rome.

   C. 2

delicious sausage, okay?

3. Which item is most likely to be found in your car's glove compartment?

A. sausages

B. box of crayons that's been melted into beautiful artifact

C. tissues, mostly unused

Answer Key:

Mostly As: Hoarder. Hoarding perishable items is gross, and it means that mold spores and other stuff are in your air and you're breathing them. Pure messiness is an art, not a health hazard. Keep your shit in check.

Mostly Bs: You're trying. Folk art is an acceptable excuse for keeping literally anything.

Mostly Cs: Not a hoarder. See page 110.

Shopping is fun

Not a hoarder? Cool, go get some more stuff. Accumulating things is an essential and healthy stage of life, if you're lucky. In Maslow's hierarchy of needs, step three involves the need for "love and belonging." Or, what he probably meant: Love and Belongings. In other words, in your quest toward enlightenment, you gotta have some stuff first. You'll never reach the mountaintop otherwise.

Your stuff journey probably looks like this:

- You move out on your own with a borrowed suitcase and your Mickey Mouse alarm clock and your shitty Chat Toulouse/ Gustav Klimt/Kurt Cobain posters.

- You get a job at a tech startup or as a waitress or working as a secretary in a doctor's office, and soon you've got money to buy a second-hand sofa and exchange your posters for some framed art.

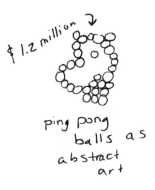

$ 1.2 million

ping pong balls as abstract art

- Maybe you move in with someone you love or who is just okay and get married and you get some new dishes or hand towels as gifts. This is long before you start Googling the phrase, "Why did I get married?" (Blame society, son!)

- You buy an apartment or house. You fill it with stuff.

- You buy a dog or cat and dress it up in tiny coats.

dog wearing a sweater

- You birth a baby and buy the baby stuff.

- Your parents downsize their house and you take a shit ton of stuff from them, like an old lamp you've always loved and 40 boxes of your childhood things they were storing in their basement, and a few china figurines.

- Pretty soon you're looking at downsizing your *own* house because the kids are grown and the stairs are a problem and wouldn't

it be nice to own a condo in Clearwater
instead of shoveling snow every winter like
an asshole?

Anyway—let's get back to that earlier stage in
life where you're getting more stuff. The Love
and Belongings stage. This is literally the best
stage of your life. Don't ruin it by embracing
some bullshit minimalist fad. There are many
people who never even reach this stage, people
without the opportunity to continually accu-
mulate things—people who have struggled with
homelessness or refugees who've had to leave

everything behind. My aunt was working as a nurse in Nigeria when the civil war broke out in 1967. She and her new husband had to flee the country with just one suitcase each—she chose to take her wedding album. Luckily they're still married and she's not berating herself for taking the photos and leaving behind her collection of gold bullion or whatever. You owe it to her to buy more stuff online.

So first, be grateful for what you already have and the fact that your new pair of sneakers is a small step on the path to enlightenment. What do you own that is fucking awesome? What about the edgy ink sketch of a penis you got framed? Vampy lipstick in a gold case you only wear when you're shitfaced? A pair of socks with little sushis on them? Stolen silverware or pint glasses for your collection? We like having things, and we like getting more things. And that's okay! You're not an evil consumerist sheep. You're just a guy or gal who likes the look of that vintage

Assorted trendy pillows

sweater and who thinks it might be nice to own. Look, it's 10 bucks. A pretty good deal. Try enjoy the experience of purchasing that sweater and let go of the guilt associated with knowing that you have a shit ton of sweaters already. So what? You like and want this one. A good way to tell if you should buy something is to ask yourself: Do I want it? If the answer is yes, then buy it. Whatever it is. Life is short and you've earned it. You're a nice person, probably, just doing your best. Make things a little easier on yourself and buy some shit you don't need. You're welcome! Even better, once you've mastered this stage of life, the next stage is all about bins full of puppies.

In conclusion

"To be yourself in a world that is constantly trying to make you something else is the greatest accomplishment."
—RALPH WALDO EMERSON

By now you've realized that throwing out all your
belongings isn't a viable way to properly be alive. Even if
you got rid of 90 percent of your belongings, your house
isn't going to be "clean" or tidy, even if some utter cock of
a book tells you so. If you've ever moved from one place
to another you can visualize what I mean. The movers
(a.k.a. your friends you're paying in beer who secretly
hate you right now) leave, and your place is still somehow
filled with stuff—old extension cords, paperclips, dust
bunnies, the warranty booklet for the microwave—bits
of debris and detritus from the life of the house. It's like
your suitcase after you've been on vacation a few days.
A little clothing bomb went off and fucked your shit up
into wrinkled piles while you were out rubbing up on
your scuba instructor in the hotel hot tub. Whatever.
You were way too busy enjoying unlimited frozen rum
cocktails from the pool bar to put your shit in hotel
drawers that probably had bedbugs anyway.

I understand the appeal of throwing stuff away
and getting back to basics. I get it. There's a reason people take vacations in geo domes in the

California desert that run on solar power and contain only the necessities so they can then Instagram it insufferably. It's nice to get away from it all and not worry about tidying and concern yourself only with the latest cougar sighting while watching for aliens. It's trendy to be minimalist these days. But escaping our homes is not the answer, nor is throwing stuff away. It's about living now with what we have and giving ourselves permission to be messy, slightly untidy, busy-as-fuck normal human beings.

Take a moment now to congratulate yourself on getting this far. In life. You're alive and reading and/or skimming a book. Not bad. Not a terrible place to be at the moment. You're as close as you've ever been to living a fuller and more exciting life where something like skydiving or buying a 60-dollar candle no longer sounds so crazy. I can't make you love your mess any more than someone can make you tidy by telling you to give away all your shit. No one can make you do anything you don't want to do, really. Although if you read up on MKUltra and the US government experiments with mind control, it's a super interesting thing to consider. The Unabomber, for example, was a volunteer at Harvard for a secret sociological study on mind control funded by the military. So was Whitey Bulger. If that sounds too Jesse Ventura or the-earth-is-flat for you, look that shit up. You have time, now that you're not freaking out about tidying anymore. The point is, it's up to you to stop giving a fuck. Unless it isn't. Maybe I'm in the employ of the Federal Shopping Consortium and this whole book is designed to make you buy things to help stimulate the economy, like when George W. Bush told everyone to go shopping after 9/11. Maybe all those other authors encouraging you to throw stuff away and live frugally are on some kind of government list of anti-capitalist communist agitators. We'll never know. We do know that to live your best life you should buy a bunch of copies of this book for your friends. Have more. Store it on the floor. Break FREE.

Resources

The acquiring of more stuff is a wonderful, fulfilling journey. Here are some places to help get you started:

ETSY

This is a big one. Support artists around the world by purchasing cement soap dispensers, copper cocktail shakers, macramé wall hangings, natural deodorant, and literally anything else people can make with their hands.

BOOKSTORES

These are great, even if you're not super into reading, because these days bookstores stock everything from onesies (My Mommy Loves Jane Austen) to mugs to candles to blankets. For this reason, they're a great one-stop shop for last-minute birthday gifts. Grab some book-themed home goods (bookends in the shape of the letters A and Z, for example) along with the latest book of cat poetry, and show your friends you love them.

EBAY

This is basically like the world's biggest garage sale.
Hey, I love this slightly used purse. Would you take three
dollars for it? No? Four? Five? This is a good way to
spend your entire day at work. Just bidding on various items you definitely need while answering one
out of seven work emails to let people know you're at
your desk but super busy.

ONLINE RETAILERS

People get all butt-hurt about these sites because
they're killing mom-and-pop stores and the workers
are all paid two dollars an hour with no bathroom
breaks. But people shop at them because they can
buy their shampoo, a new microfiber couch, cat food,
a cruise-appropriate maxi dress, and four hundred
adult coloring books and have that shit at their
house two days later. Sorry, other stores.

Clutter checklist

Here's a handy checklist to consult to ensure you're maximizing your clutter potential. Any one of these items in your home or workspace shows you're on the right track.

- ❑ Die-cut Post-it notes in the shape of hearts, cats, or arrows

- ❑ Mug that says "I Have the Same Number of Seconds in the Day as Beyoncé"

- ❑ Gold letterpress poster that says HUSTLE

- ❑ Wine charms

- ❑ Terrarium

- ❑ Spider plant

- ❑ Stones from a beach that you collected on vacation somewhere warm

- ❑ Recycled bourbon bottle used as a vase

- ❑ Cheese knife

- ❑ Bike helmet

- ❑ Four or more vibrators

- ❑ Water gun for spraying the cats or ferrets when they're bad

- ❑ Dried flowers from prom or wedding

- ❑ One item of jewelry you will never wear but it belonged to a relative and has sentimental value

- ❑ A tie clip or belt buckle owned by your grandfather

- ❑ A china plate owned by your grandmother

- ❑ A small doll made out of cat lint

- ❑ High heels you can't wear anymore because of your back issues

- ❏ A hot pair of shoes that don't fit and give you blisters

- ❏ More than four books you haven't read but have owned for more than a year

- ❏ An old-timey analog radio

- ❏ More than two throw pillows

- ❏ A ceramic object in the shape of something like a house or a tulip

- ❏ A beer stein you got in Germany

- ❏ A pint glass you stole from a bar

- ❏ A container full of spare change

- ❏ Comic books that will definitely let you retire early when you sell them

- ❏ A drawer just for stationery

pebble
collection

❑ A Christmas ornament from your childhood

❑ Seasonal lip gloss or lipstick (plum for fall,
red for winter, pink for spring, coral for
summer)

❑ A chalkboard or anything covered in chalkboard paint

❑ A craft made out of a mason jar (congrats
on your Pinterest account)

❑ More than four remote controls with a
million buttons that make no sense. Wasn't
everything supposed to be voice activated by
now? The future has really let us all down.

❑ A drawer of USB cables and old cellphones

❑ A fridge covered in wedding invitations, baby photos, and coupons along with 10 or more novelty magnets

❑ A box of art supplies filled with pencil crayons, oil pastels, water colors, sketchbooks, and paintbrushes for your once-a-year "I'm going to be more creative" phase

❑ A set of weights in red, turquoise, or pink

acknowledgments

Thanks to my editor Ann Treistman and to Sarah Bennett at The Countryman Press. Thanks to everyone in marketing, sales, and publicity at W. W. Norton. Thanks, booze.